READ, THINK, PRAY, DO

a kid's guide to reading the Bible

Written by SIMON CAMILLERI
Illustrated by DOMINIC ON

**Dedicated to my wife Catherine,
who encouraged and inspired
our Family Bible Time over the years.**

Printed in the UK.
ISBN: 978-1-83728-040-7

Published by 10Publishing, a division of 10ofThose Limited, Tomlinson Road, Leyland, Lancs, PR25 2DY, England

info@10ofthose.com www.10ofthose.com

1 3 5 7 9 10 8 6 4 2

A GROWN-UP'S GUIDE TO THIS BOOK

The idea of encouraging your kids to read the Bible may feel like a daunting task. Some presume their kids will not be able to pay attention or that it will be too confusing. You might also feel personally ill-equipped to lead them through the Scriptures. Even as adults, we can struggle to read the Bible for ourselves, so how do we teach our children to do it?

This book is a simple and kid-friendly guide to reading God's word with your children. It will introduce them to four easy steps: READING the Bible, THINKING about what it means, PRAYING about what we've learned and DOING what it teaches. Read, think, pray, do.

As you will discover, this book has two sections. Firstly, read and enjoy the illustrated story with your children and then it's time to open up the Bible together. Use the questions and ideas in the second half of this book to guide your kids through a passage of Scripture.

You can also find more creative ideas and resources at: www.kidsguidebooks.com

The Bible is a special book.

You might think
only grown-ups read it,

but kids just like you
also need it.

If you can read (or be read to)
then God's word is a word for you.

But it's so BIG!
It looks so hard!

What do you do?
Where do you start?

Well let me share this easy guide.

Four simple steps
to keep in mind:

Let me explain each one to you.

READ

The Bible will not read itself,
so firstly, take it off the shelf.

Open it up and you'll discover
sixty-six books inside its cover!

There's POETRY, PHILOSOPHY, LETTERS, LAWS and PROPHECY!

The whole thing tells an epic story
of God's love and grace and glory!

At first its SIZE might make you scared,
but pick a book and just start there.

Ask God to help you as you start
with ears to hear and open heart.

And as it's read (or as it's heard)
remind yourself: THIS IS GOD'S WORD.

THINK

Now that you've read:
Good Job! Well done!
But reading words is just step one.

God wants you now to use your head.
To think about the words you've read.

WONDER PONDER MEDITATE
CONTEMPLATE! INVESTIGATE!

If you have questions, big or small,
You should feel free to ask them all.

If it's confusing, don't feel bad.
Just talk it through with mum or dad.

God gave you an amazing brain,
so think and read and think again.

And as you think and as you read,
ask God for the wisdom that you need.

PRAY

Once you've thought through what it's saying,
the next step is to spend time praying.

God has spoken to you and I,
and prayer is how you now reply.

Tell God of all
that you have learned,

the parts that left
your heart concerned,

the bits you loved
or left you reeling...

Tell God whatever you are feeling.

Pray "WOW GOD"
when it prompts your praises.

Pray "THANK YOU"
when God's grace amazes.

Pray "SORRY"
when God shows your sin.

Pray "PLEASE"
to cast your cares on Him.

God will hear the words you say,
so read God's word, then think, then pray.

DO

Now you might think it all stops there.
You've read, you've thought, you've said a prayer.

You've done so much, there's no more to it...

Well not so fast!

Now you must
DO IT!

You can't just read and think and pray
then simply put God's word away.

You must respond! Your life should change!
If it did not, that would be strange.

So let the Bible have impact.
Don't just read, decide to act!

And get excited when you read –
To hear His voice and His voice heed.

To let His word be a word to you.
To READ and THINK and PRAY and DO.

So there we go! That's my four steps.
I hope you found them helpful tips.

I hope you see it's not too hard.
Just ask someone to help you start.

Then open it up
and follow this guide.

Who knows what treasures lie inside?

Who knows what God
might have to say?

So why not read
God's word today?

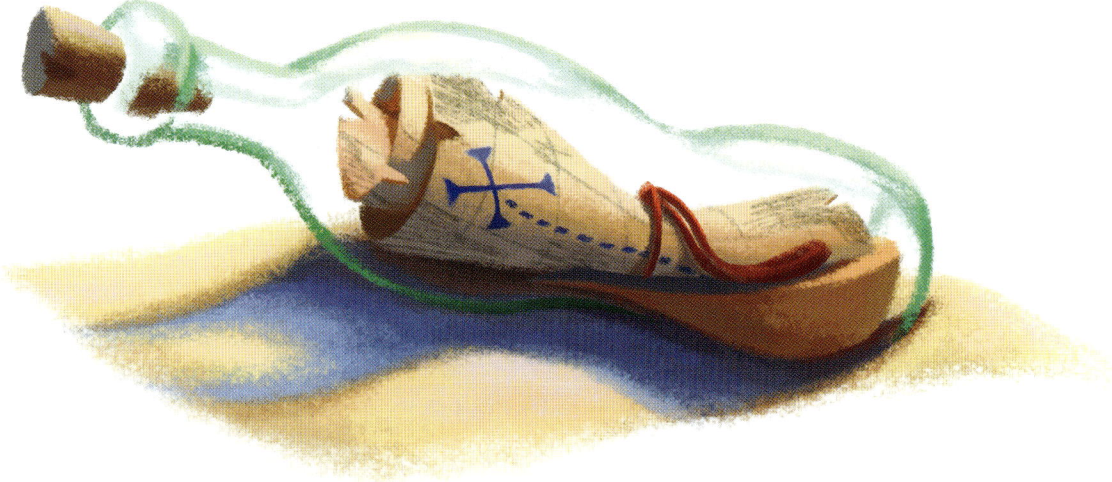

TIME TO READ!

The next few pages are written to guide you through the four steps as you read a passage of the Bible.

New to reading the Bible? Don't know where to begin?
I recommend you find the first four books of the New Testament.
These are called "gospels" and are titled Matthew, Mark, Luke and John.
The gospels are a great way of being introduced
to who Jesus is, what he taught and what he came to do.

So choose a gospel (or any other book in the Bible) and start there.
You don't have to read much at all. You could read one chapter,
or one smaller story, or even just one paragraph.
Also, if you are a kid, I recommend reading with a grown-up,
as they can help you along the way.

Hey grown-ups! For more creative ideas go to: www.kidsguidebooks.com

READ the Bible

What Bible passage have you decided to read?

Before you begin, it's helpful to have a piece of paper, a notebook or even a whiteboard with you.

As you read through the passage, engage with it in fun and creative ways!

Suggestions

- WRITE DOWN WHAT YOU OBSERVE.
- DRAW WHAT'S BEING TALKED ABOUT.
- RECREATE IT WITH TOYS OR CRAFT.
- ACT IT OUT WITH COSTUMES AND PROPS.

Warning! This can get silly.

"God has breathed life into all Scripture. It is useful for teaching us what is true. It is useful for correcting our mistakes. It is useful for making our lives whole again. It is useful for training us to do what is right."

(2 TIMOTHY 3:16)

THINK about it

What are your thoughts about what the passage means?

Does your passage have any tricky words?

What questions do you have? Write them all down!

What does it teach you about God, about yourself or about the world?

It's ok if you don't have all the answers!

"Lord, I really love your law! All day long I spend time thinking about it. Your commands make me wiser than my enemies, because your commands are always in my heart. I know more than all my teachers do, because I spend time thinking about your covenant laws."

(PSALM 119:97–99)

PRAY about it

Talk to God in prayer about all that you have learned from your Bible passage.

WOW GOD!
What in your passage inspires you to praise God?

THANK YOU
What leads you to thank God?

SORRY
Does anything point out your sin and lead you to apologise to God?

PLEASE
Finally, ask God to help you believe it and live it out.

"Take the sword of the Holy Spirit. The sword is God's word. At all times, pray by the power of the Spirit. Pray all kinds of prayers. Be watchful, so that you can pray. Always keep on praying for all the Lord's people."
(EPHESIANS 6:17–18)